PICTURE ME
My 3 and me

Anna Binks

*Your imagination is the trailer of
your own real life movie*

Introduction

You may find this a strange book.

It is a book of real experience, real life and it is one of hope of the future. I figure that if I write it down as well as visualise it, then it may help it come true. Isn't that what manifesting is?!

It's a book of thanks, to the ones who have been there for us. Our gang - Tents & Mobile Homes, Potterdale Pals, Andrea, Lou, Lauren, Tiny, Hayley, Nicola, Granno, Claire, Rachel, Rachael, Jane, Kelly, JB, Stephen, Linda, Wendy P, Pauline, Tess and all those in the background who are genuinely rooting for us. My little brothers, who too have been through far too much loss, and who I still want to protect.

It's a book with words that may help someone going through similar or may be watching someone go through similar.

And it is a book so that my husband and children always know that it is them who gets me through the hurdles.

Them that I focus on, them that give me hope and the urge to keep up the good fight.

So, to Phil, Esme and Jacob…

…always know you are loved.
Always know you have given me the best life.
I love making memories with you and I hope that
if there is ever a time I am not with you,
that my love, values and morals will be instilled deep within you.

"I would find you, in any lifetime. I would find you and love you longer".

PICTURE ME

Because my husband read this in advance and told me he was confused, this may assist....

The chapters written in *italic* are my hopes, visualisation and manifesting of the future. There are some real life elements in here too. I am writing it as if I am there already, in the future.

The other chapters in just plain old normal are my real life experience of this sh!t show called cancer.

I am a novice at this. At the writing. At using the apps associated with writing a book and uploading it so please skim over the mistakes.

My lovely little gang and I have always done good to others. Raising money for cancer charities, brain tumour charities. Shoe box appeals. Donating to gofundme's and strangers personal plights which have torn at our heart strings.

I am very aware that the cost of living crisis is real. People don't have the money to support everything. And people want something for their money. Here, I am admitting I am being selfish. I am no J K Rowling so don't expect to sell many copies of this book. But, any monies raised will go towards making memories with my 3. So thank you in advance for your purchase. I hope you get something from this book and the many ramblings of my dodgy brain.

Picture Me

It's here.

The house is spotlessly tidy.

The kitchen isn't what it was like back then. I don't just mean the aesthetics but the overflowing goodie cupboards, to keep the never full tummies happy, are now neat and tidy. The greasy finger marks on the high gloss doors don't exist but are replaced with coffee bean spillages from Phil. The cushions on the floor from the dog sneaking onto the sofa and getting comfy are no more, he neither has the agility or inclination to leap. The many pots from hard welded on Weetabix suppers are replaced by last night's remnants of the rum and coke shared by dad and daughter long after I went to bed.

It's 5am. Still night time in my book but the sun is shining through the vast glass doors and I am confused by what I am feeling. Today is a goal I have had for 18 years. The goal that has kept me focussed on even the bleakest of days. I visualised it so much that I could hear it, I could see it, I could smell it and my heart could definitely feel it. The anticipation, the excitement, the sense of achievement and also a little fear now that my goal has finally come around.

I sit with my coffee looking out across the garden. I have done this many times across the years and all the "it feels like yesterday" floods through my brain. But it really does feel like yesterday. Laying on the bed and talking to her as she grew in my tummy. Sitting watching her and listening to those little baby breath noises. Sobbing on my bedroom floor because her daddy had moved her into her nursery whilst I had nipped out to the supermarket. Bringing her perfect baby brother home on New Years Eve and eating Chinese food with special friends at a grotty wallpapering table in the almost ready extension we had built. Our girls running wild. Christmas morning trying to keep them busy whilst waiting for daddy to come home from a night shift at the fire station so we could all see if santa had been. The games of hide and seek. Me and him, dancing together with little koalas clamped to our legs wanting to be involved. I can still see it and I can still feel it.

I hear the stair squeak and she walks in to a wet eyed smiling mother. "I knew you'd do this" she exclaims as she comes to join me on the sofa. "Once we have got our make up done, we are NOT crying" she says very unconvincingly. She lays her head on my lap and I begin to stroke her hair. She still wakes up looking like a monkey has been playing with her hair all night. I twiddle with the baby curls at her temples which she struggles to reach with the straighteners. Her tears begin to fall onto my pyjama bottoms, "what if I'm no good at being a wife Mum?" she asks. I laugh. Our family has never ever been perfect. She must know this. I remind her. "Nothing is ever perfect, no one is ever perfect. Sometimes we are good, sometimes we are not so good but we all find our own version of perfect eventually. You and Tom have already begun to create yours".

"You and Dad made it look easy though. You still do. Me and Jakes were always with you, 24/7 and always so happy Mum". I swallow the lump in my throat "you are wearing those rose tinted specs again Es. It has NEVER ever been easy for us. Work, health, family. Never easy. But you know what got us through the hard times… Love. Our love for one another. Our love for you and your brother. We tried to protect you from the really hard times but it's because of those times that we are the family that we are. Far from text book perfect that's for sure". She bites her lip. "I know it was hard sometimes Mum. I saw you so many times. Keeping hold of things for our memory boxes. Those photo albums you always did with everything written down of what we were doing. I knew you were scared Mum".

"I never wanted you to wonder Esme. I wanted you to know how loved and wanted you and Jacob were and if there was a time I wasn't here, I wanted to try and make sure you had all the answers to your questions in case you didn't have me here to answer them".

"Busy Binks. That's what some of my friends called me. The holidays we had. The walks on the beach in all weathers. The nights in the bar. And when we turned off our phones to just sit and watch films together. We were always busy…busy doing something or doing nothing." She said smiling.

"We were. And you were that used to it that you would ask all the time what are we doing this weekend before the one we were still in was over. Jacob even used to tell me that I had to consult with him if I was thinking about making plans for us all! Nine years old, cheeky little shite".

We sit together reminiscing, a few tears but many more smiles and before we know it, it's 7am. The caterers have adorned the island with a feast that looks far too pretty to eat. Phil walks in "Bloody hell, how much is all this costing me?" he says. "I could have put a few slices of bread in the toaster". She laughs and teases him, "wait til the girls all get here Dad. The leccy app will be going off like the clappers". I remembered the days of him checking his app to see how much energy I was using while he was at work. If he was late I would run around the house putting the dishwasher, washer and drier on along with the oven to start tea and wait for him to see the energy surge so he would get a wiggle on and get home to us! He loves a full house. And he loves feeding people just as much as I do so I know he's teasing.

The girls she refers to are the girls who have enjoyed our home with us for many years. There is Evie; the one who is family. Besties with her parents. Where the Boswell's were, the Binks were. We had, and still have, some great holidays with them. I still miss watching them come into the room after making up dance routines and performing them for us. There is Millie; the primary school bestie with a knack for tidying and organising. How I loved that girl coming over. She always rearranged Esme's room and did a much better job than I could ever do. Rose. The curly haired dinky dot who knew her own mind from the start. And there is Frankie; the lovely girl she met at University who has never failed to turn up and see us on Christmas Eve. Along with the Chapman's a few doors up... Frankie ended up falling head over heels in love with Josh at one of our festive gatherings and since then they have been inseparable.

Esme wanted her last night as a Miss to be spent with just us and Jacob, her little brother, well in age but not in stature. He's still in bed. He had gone to the local with Tom and the rest of his grooms men last night. And in true, little lads at heart fashion, the very merry feeling washed over them and they thought it was a good idea to head to the casino until the very early hours. Now there was many a time that Phil used to do the same in his younger years. The nights I would erupt at him because he hadn't taken a key and I would either be awake terrified that the door was unlocked and someone could walk in, or I wouldn't be able to sleep because I knew that at some point he would be knocking at the door and potentially be waking up two little ones. Either way he was in trouble.

It wasn't long before he started to use the line "nothing good happens after midnight" and those testosterone fuelled nights became a distant memory as he settled into middle age. The truth really was that he couldn't be arsed hanging around in the cold waiting for a taxi to our little village, so he ended up building his own bar at home. And didn't everyone know about it. He invited everyone at least once. He would welcome guests with open arms. He dressed up as father Christmas one year and had me buying gifts for the whole street. The kids knew how to pour a pint at 7 and 9 years old. We had burly fire fighters fall asleep spooning on the bar sofa, we had them putting the bbq on at 4am when they got a second wind. And we also had lots of time in there just us 4. It was a god send during the pandemic all those years ago. I bloody loved that first lock down. Before it we could be like ships passing in the night, juggling work, school, clubs, parties and everything else in between. And then all those interruptions had gone and we had work to go to (key workers we were!) and home. It was bloody lovely. Playing go fish, playing the ministers cat, snuggling on the sofa watching a film or dancing and singing our favourite songs. Probably why still to this day Jacob enjoys all the old songs.

"Morning sis" Jacob hoarsely says as he comes and joins us in the kitchen. He heads to the coffee machine. "Wow Tom was on fire last night Es. Some leggy redhead was all over him...Ill be surprised if he turns up for you today you know".

She points to her fluffy bed socks and messy hair "he likes the homely look, he will be there". "But you look homeless sis not homely". He walks over to her and kisses her head. "I can't believe my big sis is getting married" he says. "Finally I get a brother".

My heart feels insanely happy having us all under the same roof. Even if they do still bicker. God, it used to drive me insane. I always thought I would be one of those perfect mums. No processed foods, reward charts that worked, no shouting. Instead they were brought up on love, laughter and a few profanities along the way. Summers in the garden, paddling pool out, water fights and making our own fun. The neighbours could hear the shrieking, laughter and screeching, from 4 doors up. That's how we became friends actually. We used to just walk past one another on the school run, do that awkward smile you do when passing people and say hello. Then I heard some shrieking and screeching from her house one day and thought "I want to be her friend". She was like me in a way. If she wasn't feeling it she would retreat. Menopausal she would say, or rather her husband Craig said. She was the most selfless person I had ever met. As they say "chance made us neighbours, trips to b&m, lunches out and long nights chatting in the bar made us friends". I know, 'they' didn't say it. I did.

Talking of neighbours, they just walk in. I knew there was no way Frankie would be walking down to us by herself. If one Chapman comes, all of them turn up! Josh, with as much bouncing enthusiasm for life as he had at 11 years old, flies through the door singing going to the chapel. Craig follows with 2 cold bottles of stella and asks if we have a fuse he can borrow. The times I would wonder where Phil had got to when he was walking the dog and I would get a photo of him sat opposite craig at their kitchen table with a cold beer and the spare fuse sat there for decoration. And then in walks H. She heads straight over to me "you alright Mrs" she whispers with tears in her eyes. "Big day for you little mama" she says to me while gently squeezing my hand. She turns to look for Esme "there she is, my beautiful bride. Come on, bring it in girl". Esme does not need telling twice, she has always enjoyed a Helen hug. And has always called her second mama. Not an ounce of jealousy from me about that statement. Helen and I never even had to have the direct conversation. I just knew that she would always be there for my babies... no matter how old they get.

I can hear Frankie on the phone and she rushes to the door. The girls have arrived. Jacob and Phil both give me a kiss and they head out of *the way and up to the Chapman's where their dapper wedding attire awaits. Esme didn't want either of them to see her getting ready.*

I told her many years ago that during my bleak days I would visualise her standing in her dress. Her dad looking at her for the first time with Jacob stood behind him. My brain held every detail. All of the noises fading into the background. The smell of her special wedding day perfume. The swoosh of her dress as she makes the way to her Dad. My perfectly imperfect family. It made me smile most of the time, but sob on the days when the intrusive thoughts were just too much and would terrify me that I wouldn't get to see it.

Change

9 April 2021

"Come home. It's changed" I faltered as he answered my call. "I'm on my way".

He didn't need to hear or say anything else. He just knew in my voice. I'd been having these MRI's since 2010. Only in the lead up to this one, we knew deep down inside there was a difference. The thunderclap headaches which made me writhe around in pain and unable to sleep. The vomiting each morning and definitely not from a baby growing after my recent hysterectomy. One night in particular was excruciating, and with hindsight, I should have gone into A&E but the pandemic was still on and I was reluctant to add to their pressures. So now, I sit here on the big sofa rocking back and forth looking out of the window for him.

I should have known this was coming. A few weeks ago at work, as we celebrated the retirement of one of our much loved consultants, I was eating canapes and chatting to Dr M a neurologist from the medical group I worked in. My manager Stephen had asked him to see me as he could see I was suffering with headaches. Dr M prescribed me some some pills to tide me over until the mri results were in. As we schmoozed in the boardroom, he asked how I was doing and whether I had received the results. When I said I hadn't, he told me he would check for me before our Webex meeting. I listened to all of the wonderful speeches and then headed back to the office with nervous energy bubbling in my tummy. As I logged on, I saw Dr M. "Anna, remind me of your date of birth" "5th April 1979. Thank you so much for doing this" I babbled. "I might be able to get some sleep now". And then I read his face. I could see his eyes reading the report and then very quickly he looked up and said it hadn't been reported yet. Again, I thanked him for looking and we muted our screens waiting for the others to join the actual meeting. By this time my manager had arrived back from the boardroom and I heard her take a call. She told my colleague to start without her as Dr M had asked her to pop upstairs to see him. I knew. I KNEW. Of course I told Phil when I got home and he said I was being daft and reading into things. But, I KNEW! I had seen these reports for patients before. At the bottom it reads something similar to "URGENT. This report contains significant radiological findings requiring prompt attention". I was convinced that was what he had read.

And when, on 9 April 2021, my phone rang from a withheld number I answered it knowing it was the hospital. I had just driven into our pretty little village and parked outside our house. The house that had known mostly happy times. The house where there had been far more laughs than tears. Holly, the Neuro Oncology Nurse Specialist said hello and then said that the results were back. She began to tell me that the neurosurgeon would call me on Monday. It is hard to read the nurses voices. They are empathetic anyway and the situation isn't great no matter what so they've rarely been jolly on the phone. "How much do you want to know Anna" she asked with a gentle voice. "I need to know Holly, I can't spend the weekend with my imagination running wild. I mean, do I need Phil to be with me on Monday?" I asked. "It would be a good idea to have your husband with you Anna" she replied in an almost apologetic voice. She went on to tell me that the little birth mark that was found in my brain during a completely unrelated scan back in 2010, was now definitely not a birth mark. It had never been biopsied due to the position and it being so deep in my brain, but advances in imaging had shown that it was a tumour. And more worryingly, it had grown by a third. Prior to this call they had already met at their weekly multi disciplinary meeting where very brainy brain specialists sat around the table looking at my noggin and had decided that surgery was the best option. Even though 'I KNEW IT' I was still in shock. My body began to shake. I felt sick. I mean, my family history of cancer was huge. I had been with my parents supporting them being given their diagnosis and beyond but to be the patient myself was another level.

All I could think about was my babies. I was due to pick Esme and Jacob from school any minute. I rang my friend sobbing. She didn't even ask anything she just said I will get them and keep them busy until you are ready.

I was on auto pilot. I rang the school to give permission for Claire to collect the children. Mrs Henderson, a petite delicate lady who is so caring and gentle, answered and then she asked me if I was ok. I could barely speak. Goodness knows what she must have thought. I felt terrible that I must have upset her weekend.

I was still sat rocking on the sofa and saw him pull up on the drive. My stocky 6ft4 husband in a tiny white Vauxhall corsa we had as a little run around. I couldn't even get up from the sofa my legs were like jelly. The door opened and there he was filling the entire doorway – white as snow with tears falling onto his cheeks. "I can't lose you. I can't lose you" he repeated. We sat and we cried. He listened to me telling him what Hannah had said. And he didn't interrupt. Very unlike my Phil as he always has something to say and often says it whilst you're mid-sentence. The weekend went by in an absolute blur. Esme, 8 at the time, and Jacob 6, didn't suspect a thing. I was adamant they would continue to be children. And to have a childhood. Until we knew for sure what we were dealing with, I wanted them to be none the wiser. It's weird, I almost wished the weekend away so I could just get that call and know what we were dealing with. I do so much better with anything when I know what I am dealing with. The element of surprise has never sat well with me. I was guilty of unwrapping Christmas gifts as a child just to see what I had on the big day!

Monday came. No surprise that I had not slept well at all. Holly's call going over in my mind. I showered. I paced. I fidgeted. I had my notebook and pen ready. I had written a list of questions.

I'd put a candle on to try to chill me out. I had the house phone and my mobile in my hand. I had forgotten to ask which phone the neurosurgeon would call. And then it rang. "Quick quick" I shouted to Phil. He ran through and we sat there on the sofa, stiff as boards listening intently whilst staring into space.

Mr A is a very likeable surgeon. He introduced himself, confirmed who I was and also clarified what I was aware of so far. He explained again that the tumour had grown by a third. That I needed more in-depth scans and told me that these would plot the surgery routes and areas to avoid during the operation. I was so confused to hear this as when I had been told it was perhaps a birth mark all those years ago, they had said they couldn't biopsy as it was too dangerous yet here we were planning for major surgery. Taking my lid off so to speak. I had lots of questions. To be told this news over the phone was so difficult. I was unable to read his face or body language. I hate talking on the phone at the best of times and I had to really pay attention. I like to be organised and asked from my list of questions for much further along the line information "Anna, Anna" he interrupted "Im just the technician." He said softly. "Your oncologist will be able to answer those questions". My Oncologist? I didnt want an Oncologist. And that was it, my life, our lives had changed.

First Glimpse

Jacob is helping the bridesmaids into the cars. Esme is in her old room catching her breath. He walks in the front door. The front door with the huge step because he built it to his size! I'm stood at the bottom of the stairs. Halfway between going up to my baby girl and halfway between seeing the love of my life all dressed up for one of the most important day of his life, of our lives. He steps in the door and sees me and his hand immediately goes to his mouth. He turns away from me and leans against the door he has just closed. "Thank you" he whispers. "Thank you for everything – for this home, for us, our family". The tears sting my eyes as I head towards him. "Don't be daft thanking me. You've given me everything I ever dreamed of. Beyond what my dreams were. You made our home with your hands" I told him. "And you, you made our home with your heart Anna.". I forget that the photographer is here. I hear a click as I wipe away the gloss from his lips and look across to the man with a camera with a single tear slowly rolling down his cheek. "Bloody hell, didn't think I would be crying today" he says! All 3 of us clear our throats and then I hear her.

"Mum". You always know the tone of your child's voice. If it's a Mum he's nicked my phone, Mum can you bring me something up, Mum where's my coat, Mum what's for tea call. This was a cross between a Mum I'm scared and excited bellow. She used to struggle to know at times if she was scared or excited when there was stuff going on at school. But that always involved her sitting on the toilet with the door wide open talking to me working things out in her head. "I just feel so much better when I share my worries with you Mummy". What a bloody privilege that felt like to hear. I never ever turned her away or told her I was busy. I never shouted at her for pissing about at bedtime back and forth to the bathroom, back and forth to me. If she could simply talk to me and feel better, then I would listen. Not just give yes or no answers but really listen. And help her to answer her own questions and reach her own conclusions. I get to her room and she's twizzling her blanky. The muslin cloth she had as a baby. The muslin

cloth that got thrown in a drawer when her mates came for sleepovers and dragged out when they left and she was in the midst of her lack of sleep hangover. "Is he ok?" she asks quietly. "He's ok baby." I reply. "Thank you Mum." She begins. "Esme Eliana. Our makeup is done! Don't". I whisper as I face her and take hold of both of her hands. The sight of my little girl, now a beautiful young woman who stands before me. "My god Es, you look amazing. How...." "How did I get so lucky to be your mum" she replies laughing. "Am I that predictable" I say smiling at her. "I've only heard it every day for the last 27 years Mum" she replies. "Come on, let's go see your Dad" and I take her hand and lead her to the stairs.

"Philllll turn around and close your eyes" I shout. I watch my girl glide towards the top of the stairs. The stairs she once dragged her duvet down whilst full on sleepwalking. The stairs she used to thud up and down in a mood. The stairs she used to screech Muuuuuum down when Jacob was daring to step foot in her room. She turns to look at me and takes a breath. "I love you Mum". "I love you too darling" and then she steps slowly and carefully down the 17 steps, holding her stunning dress, for her Dad to see her for the first time.

"You here yet girl" he says.

"I'm here Dad" her voice falters.

He turns around, my 6foot4 strong husband. And he can't speak. His cheeks flush. He exhales several times. And he just keeps repeating "wow". She stands there looking at him smiling. "I used to tell your Mum I wanted a little girl when we first met" he tells her. He looks up at me and then back towards the blushing bride to be. His voice breaks again "Es. You will always be my little girl. Always."

As I reach them at the bottom of the stairs where they are still embracing, Jacob appears. He is gazing towards his feet, a tear drips down onto his very polished shoe. "I love us" he says. We all huddle and cuddle. And then normality slips back in "Jacob, your friggin corsage nearly had my eye out" she yells. Perfectly imperfect I think to *myself with a smile.*

Rocky Road

I had protected them from so much. Too much some people might say. They were 6 and 8 when it all started happening. That phone call that changed the direction of our lives. "Mummy has got a lump in her head and it shouldn't be there" I told them gently. "I have to go to hospital for a few days and have an operation". Two pairs of little eyes looked up at me. Their response? "Can we watch a film together now please Mummy". And we did just that. When they were tucked up later that night, I told Phil we would try to follow their lead. Use different opportunities to get little bits of information in. Adverts for Macmillan. Story lines on films. I somehow wanted to get information in about the situation in as gently as possible without the major, "sit on the sofa we have something to tell you" and terrifying them. It was hard, people asked questions in front of them. Or announced cancer deaths. I couldn't believe how blasé some people could be. I figured they had never had the misfortune of having serious illness within their family and that they didn't appreciate how terrifying it all was. But we got through it. I spoke to trauma counsellors to find out how to manage things for the kids. They all had their own ideas. You can't click with everyone but one particular woman stood out. Amy Irving. I liked her even from just an email and a short conversation. Her focus was on the children. Our home had always been a happy home. Just as everyone's home should be. A place of safety. That cosy warm feeling. Everyone else had told me to tell them the severity of my health at home. I didn't want to! I didn't want to spoil their safe place which was full of happy memories. Amy, without me even telling her that, talked to me about how different boys and girls are. It was like she knew my two without even meeting them. Girls often like colouring or reading to decompress. Boys like to be a bit more physical. Kicking a ball about. She told me to keep our home that safe, warm place full of happy memories. To drip feed information in as and when the opportunity arose. If we had to tell them about big things she suggested going for a walk somewhere. Some place where we could all scream and shout and get it all out. We could soak in the fresh air. Skim stones across the sea or pick flowers in the woods. Run about with Teddy.

Esme. Every night for many weeks, months even, bedtime brought out all the anxieties. We would sit on the toilet, have a sick bowl next to the bed, she would be physically shivering. I'd lay on her bed not doing anything but being there. "I always feel better when I talk to you Mummy" she would say and inside my heart pleaded with God, whoever was out there, to always let me be there for her to unload her worries to.

Jacob. We had days off school "I'm scared in case you die while I'm at school". We had very scary night terrors. I hated myself. Hated that it was my diagnosis doing this to them. They didn't really understand. Even when I thought they did. We were at the dentist completing the standard health questionnaire for me and the kids. Esme sat beside me as I went on to mine. "Wait. You've got cancer?" she said as she looked at the tick I had made in the box. "Yes darling. I've got that lump in my head remember". "But people with cancer die Mum." "Sometimes they do Es" I gently replied, "Well are you going to die Mum?" "I hope not darling. I will do everything I can not to." "You hope not?!!! Mum!!!!" she shrieked. "I am ok at the moment Esme. I promise I will tell you if there is a time that I'm not. But one thing I can tell you is that even if I do, you will be ok. We have lots of people who love you and who will look after you". That's almost word for word how that conversation went down. A mothers love is something else isn't it....I mean the way we show it. Picking up a crème egg for when they come out of school, stroking their heads, regaling stories of what we did on such a such a date. Dads tend to show their love in different ways from my experience. Fixers. Sorting the Wi-Fi out, driving us safely to places, a rub on the head and a big bear hug. I know some people think we all have a purpose in life, we are all destined to do something, aspirations for great jobs, sporting accomplishments, qualifications. Some are doctors, lawyers, save animals or teach. Me? I was meant to be Phil's wife and Esme and Jacob's mummy. And I have been bloody good at it if I do say so myself.

Surgery was booked and getting ever closer. Pre op done. The MRIs to plan the surgery route. Then just a few days before, Mr A rang me and asked me to go in. I was terrified. He didn't say much when he rang. I was far too panicked to ask anything. I thought he was going to say that they couldn't do it now. But I needed it out. Again, the not knowing, urgh just makes everything worse.

Phil knew I was scared, and I think he was too so he busied himself in the garden. So much so that when I said we had to leave he just leapt in the car with his dirty gardening clothes and crocs on. What the? Honestly, there used to be a time when people dressed up to see the doctor! I know my grandad did. Shirt and tie for a doctor's appointment. I didn't expect Phil to go in a tux but would have quite liked him not to be wearing his tatty old joggers that he had cut down to shorts because it was warm! We arrived on the 4th floor at Hull Royal. Mr A was there already waiting on the corridor. He led us to an office where we could see a scan set up on the computer screen. We knew straightaway it was me. The profile of the skull and button nose was without a doubt me, we nervously laughed. And then we saw the tumour. Visible for even us non medics to see. We both looked at one another. It was the first time we had seen Mr A in person since these results and discussions started. What was the reason we were there though? Well, he wanted to get consent for the surgery. He knew I would have to be on my own when I came to hospital on the day and it would be very overwhelming. It was a long surgery, a very big theatre slot and they needed everything to go smoothly and to be on time. He had to tell me about all of the risks. He went into a lot of detail. Phil found it really hard to listen to. He stared at his feet (well his scruffy crocs). I was on auto pilot. I could hear my own voice sounding confident almost as if it was me going to be carrying out the actual surgery. I needed to know every detail of what would happen that day and I blocked out the horrible bits. All I could focus on was getting the bastard out of my head.

Mr A explained I would come in the day before surgery and stay overnight ready for surgery early the next day. I would meet the nursing team and the rest of the surgery team and meet the physios who would help me afterwards. He said I would be in intensive care for one or two nights after the surgery and then I would go to the high dependency unit for monitoring and then the neuro ward before home. I was determined I wouldn't be in there for long. And that I would be back on the school run by the end of the week. When I had my children, I had planned c sections. I had read up on that before and it advised to get moving as soon as you could. That very day I was up and walking around and moving my body. I knew I wanted to be up and about so that I could recover well from this too. All I focussed on was getting back home.

The following few days were horrendous for me and for Phil. I was terrified I would wake up and not be the same Anna. That I wouldn't be able to be their Mum and his wife. He was terrified I would die. I was sat in the garden from 3am every day. Crying while they all slept. Poor old Ted didn't have a clue what was going on but he sat by my feet during those early hours outside. I had put all of my paperwork in order. Folders with everything in. Written down their favourite recipes and snacks they liked. Written letters to them. Ensured my funeral plan was in place and my wishes were written down. Again, auto pilot. You see death had been a part of my life from such a young age. I had found my baby sister Gemma dead in her cot when I was just six years old. It staggers me now at how grown up I was and had to be. Gemma and I had shared a room. I was like a mini mum to her; she was my real life dolly and I loved to make her laugh. But also, every morning I was up early and played with baby toys with her. So, on this particular morning when she didn't wake me up I skipped downstairs and thought to myself, I can play with my toys now until she wakes up. I've only ever dared to say that once before because I still feel guilty about it. My mum had been out the night before for a night out at the bingo. It was her first night out bless her whilst my dad was on the rigs. I played for a bit and then went to my mum's room. "Where is Gemma" she asked, I told her she was still asleep. Her face froze, her mother's intuition perhaps. "Go and get her" she told me, I instinctively knew she was scared to go in. When I went in Gemma was at the other end of her cot. Which isn't abnormal for a little wriggler. But she was very still, I put my finger under her nose and couldn't feel her warm air coming out. I was six years old. Six years old and I knew. I knew my sister was dead.

I gently lifted her out of her cot and took her to my mum "she won't wake up mummy" and my Mum let out the most awful scream I have ever heard. She took her from me and was rocking her "my baby, my baby, please, no".

I didn't know what to do, we had one of those big lumpy telephones where you had to put your finger in the circle and pull it all the way around, I dialled the only number I knew, my auntie Georgie. She must have heard my mum howling hysterically in the background and I remember screaming "she's dead auntie, Gemma's dead". The next thing I knew there was an ambulance that arrived, and they took Gemma away. I had no idea that she wouldn't come back. I thought that when you went to hospital, they made you better. My memory of the rest of the day is very blurry, I remember my Mum wasn't with us. And then suddenly my Dad walked in late at night. He was home from the rig, they had got a chopper to him and brought him home early. I was about to start telling him what had happened but before I could say anything he walked to me and kissed my head and said "I gave her a kiss bye bye from you my darling". "The hospital man is making Gemma better daddy" I cried. Tears poured down his face "she's gone". The biggest heart break any family could endure.

Still to this day I don't think that my family, not just my parents, handled us well. I was 6, Jason was 3 and Lee was 2. So the boys didn't really understand. But Jason and I would lay in bed at night together terrified if we went to sleep that it would happen to us. We took it in turns to close our eyes. I watched him like a hawk. And then he would wake up and I would sleep. No one ever actually told me Gemma was dead. They used words like 'gone', 'with the angels' and 'in heaven'. We actually lived at the side of the graveyard. I hadn't been allowed to go to the funeral. Funerals were not for children they said. But when I asked my cousin where heaven was, she said it was up in the sky and that Gemma was in the graveyard and there was a ladder which went up to heaven and Gemma climbed up it. I remember running there, frantically. I wanted my sister back. I needed to find this ladder and go up it and bring her back to us. My mum and dad would be happy again. So when I couldn't find it, again I felt such sadness.

I heard my mum once tell a friend that the day Gemma died, I went mute. I would sit alone staring into space. I barely spoke. She could hear me crying in my room. It must have been horrendous for her. But I don't remember being comforted by anyone. The family were understandably there for my mum but not us children. I guess that they thought kids are resilient, that I would forget. No one dared say Gemma's name. It was like she didn't exist. I hated it. I loved my sister. My bedroom was empty without her. And then one day my auntie Caroline came to visit from Kent. There were a lot of people in our house that day. And Auntie Caroline must have noticed me. She got down onto her knees to my level and she held my hand, she didn't even have to say anything....my face crumpled and I fled to my room in sobs. She followed me and spent so long talking to me. She asked me questions and I answered. I told her no one said Gemma's name anymore and that the ambulance man was supposed to make her better. Why didn't he? I told her I couldn't find the ladder. If I found the ladder, then I could make everyone happy again. She just held me and rocked me letting me sob into her. When it was all out, she asked me what she could do to help me. I didn't know what to say. I was just six years old. She asked me if a photograph of Gemma might help. That day I got a picture of my baby sister and I still carry it with me now. When my dad was alive he would say "I don't know how you can look at her every day. It destroys me when I see her". I was sad for him but I am also a firm believer in that we have to remember our loved lost ones, talk about them, keep their memory alive. Like that Disney film, Coco.

So, when people find it astounding that I have planned stuff and that I use some of the opportunities to speak to my children and plant seeds about what could or might happen, this is the reason why. Our minds can make up the scariest of situations. I envisaged Gemma lost in the sky, I envisaged her in the ground with worms coming out of her eyes and ears. I am determined that both of my children will feel able to ask me questions. And they will get honest, albeit gentle, answers.

When Esme asked me that day if I was going to die, I told her that I hoped not and that I would do everything possible to stay alive. I reassured her that if I did become poorly and know I was going to die then I would tell her. No matter how hard that would be for both of us. And I meant it. Every word of it. Whatever the subject, they'll be told the truth.

Mum and Son

We raise our glasses and say a family cheers together before Jacob and I head to the car. He insisted on driving me to the venue. He is in full on Jacob Russell Binks swing. My god I love this man I created. He has always been the funniest one of the family. His innuendos, one liners and twerking have never failed to make me laugh. He knew he could wrap me around his little finger and did so repeatedly over the years. He went through a short phase where it felt like I was his enemy. Wanted his own way and didnt like rules. Totally against doing anything I asked him to do and saw no reason why he should brush his teeth, get a shower, make his bed or do his homework. And then at bedtime he would want me to tuck him in. "H U G" he would spell out. And I did it. Every single time. Flick his relaxation light on, put his fan on so the cold air could blow in his face, and wrap him up in his duvet for him to then pull me in for a cuddle and kiss. I used to sneak in to see both Esme and Jacob every time I got up for a wee in the night. Mostly because I had to check they were still breathing. If I thought I would try to break the habit of going in, I then kept myself awake thinking the same would happen to them as it had done to Gemma. So I always checked them. There is nothing more beautiful than watching your children gently sleep. No matter how trying the day had been, all was forgotten when they were resting.

He opens the car door for me. "Mrs Binks" he smiles broadly. "Why thank you son" I reply. He holds my hand as I get in and then gently scoops up the skirt I am wearing and eases it into the car. He then passes me the seat belt. "Comfy Mum?" he asks before gently closing the door and scooting round to the driver's side. "Cleaned the car especially for the most important lady today Mum" he winks. "And I've even done you a little playlist". And it begins. All of the songs we have enjoyed together over the years. My eyes fill up. So many memories of us dancing to these songs in the kitchen or in the bar. The road trips. The fact that my little boy is now a grown man with the most beautiful heart. And I truly do appreciate the time and effort he has put into this.

It's a beautiful clear dry day. Just right. He's set the music volume just right – loud enough for us to sing along but quiet enough that we can still hear one another. We sing along to the tracks – Chris Stapleton, Sam Fender, Bob Seger. And we catch a glimpse of one another and smile. I can certainly feel the tears stinging my eyes and I'm pretty sure I've seen this strapping lad of mine swallow a lump in his throat a few times.

This is already my favourite day EVER.

It's a dogs life.

The day I was due to be admitted arrived. Bags were packed, fridge stocked up. I had told the kids that I would be in hospital when they got home from school but that I would facetime them. And then I gave them both huge hugs and kisses and packed them off to school. School was very much another safe space. Their teachers were amazing. I knew that they were in safe hands and that the Head Mistress and the rest of the team really cared. Esme had said to me once "what if you die and my dad gets a girlfriend who is nice to me when he's there and mean to me when he's not". I mean I wanted to say "Ill fucking haunt her" but instead reassured her that Daddy is a good judge of character but if that did happen then she can talk to auntie Jane, auntie Lauren or Helen....or her teachers. I told Miss V this conversation and straight away she backed me up and made it known that even if they were adults, the kids could always talk to her, and she would help. I just felt like I was surrounded by good people – what more could I want. Oh yeah, to live a long life.

So in between checking and double checking my bags the phone rang. It was one of the matrons from the hospital. She explained that they were struggling for a bed for me. My heart sank. I was geared up and ready for this tumour to be out now. As my job in the hospital was managing beds, I knew how hard they would be trying to avoid cancelling my surgery. Still, I was worried. She said she would keep working on it and call me back after the next bed meeting. The next bed meeting came and went, and it was even more busy so she was still struggling. The kids came home from school and were surprised to see me. I can't say I was with them in mind because my head was all over the place with everything being up in the air. And then the teatime bed meeting took place. The matron rang me again. "We aren't cancelling you but we can't admit you tonight. Have the night at home and please arrive on the ward for 7am in the morning" she said.

The whole 7am gave us problems as we didn't want to drag the kids to the hospital to drop me off. It was also a school day. Phil made a phone call to our friends Chris and Claire to ask if they could have the kids early for us so that Phil could get me to the hospital and of course, they said yes. I told the kids that they were going to the Pickering's for breakfast. They were so excited. It helped bring me back in the room and I got into my positive thinking again. I got an extra night in my own bed, or should we say the garden. I was sat in the garden at 3am and distinctly remember the dog dragging his backside along the grass and then licking his balls. Again, my perfectly imperfect family.

The morning came round quickly. I was in the bath for 5am and then started making a racket to wake everyone else up at 6am. Once the kids were dressed, I sent them downstairs to Phil so that I could catch my breath and again sort out the things I had for them. I left Phil a letter under his pillow. And I put some little gift bags out for the kids for when they got home on the evening. I know honestly, mad. But I wanted them to have something....just incase.

It was time. I headed downstairs. Bags in the car and headed round to the Pickering's. I couldn't get out of the car – the emotions were really building now. Chris and Claire knew what a big day it was. They had plans for Phil to keep him busy after he had dropped me off. Phil saw the kids inside and I gave a very feeble wave.

I feared the journey. Phil would rather take a longer route and be moving, than a shorter one and be sat at a standstill. He is renowned for this. We nearly missed our Disney Paris train years ago because of his navigating. If I ever ask him what time he will be home, I always add a good hour onto that and then I'm not as disappointed when he is late. But the traffic was surprisingly good. That ride to the hospital. Silent. Both of us. Neither of us could talk. The front of the tower block was being worked on so we pulled past the maternity hospital. Some memories there I thought.

Our two are IVF babies, we spent many a time in there. Consultations, injections, scans. He seemed to be thinking the same as he gave me a squeeze on the leg. And then he stopped the car. I told him I loved him so much. And that I would be ok. I kissed him so hard on the lips. Touched his face. Looked into his eyes. I can't explain it, the atmosphere was tense but full of love. Scared but hopeful. He went to get out of the car to get my bag but I got him to stay inside. It was still full covid rules at the hospital and I definitely didn't want him to get poorly. And if I lingered for too long I wasn't sure I would go in so I got out, got my little holiday case still with flight labels from the last trip attached to it and I began to walk. Fast. I looked back expecting to see him moving off, heading home and giving me a wave. But he was still there. Head in his hands leaning down onto the steering wheel. My heart almost broke. This is my fault. I am hurting my husband and my babies.

Magical

Just wow. We walk through the doors to the venue. People are enjoying drinks and complimenting one another on their outfits. Everything looks amazing. Everyone looks bloody amazing. The bridesmaids are hiding in another room so the guests can't see them, and awaiting Esme and Phil. Jacob heads over to Tom and I am engulfed by all my friends! Lauren (who has always kept me going with her reaffirming words), Jane, Kelly, Helen, Tracy, Andrea, Tess….so many people with their hearts full for my beautiful girl and her soon to be husband. Tom's parents arrive and we have a moment. Phil and I are so grateful she is making a life with someone who has a supportive and loving family. They have welcomed Esme as part of their family from day one. And they have welcomed us too. It all feels so bloody magical. I've got nervous excited butterflies. I already know how beautiful she looks and I cannot wait for everyone else to see her.

The Master of Ceremonies rings a delicate bell. "Ladies and gentlemen, will you please finish your drinks and head to the ceremony room". Despite being modest and not one for the limelight, Esme has planned this day meticulously. We all know where we are supposed to be and when. Tom and his best man will walk in once everyone is seated. Tom's parents will walk in together. Followed by Jacob and I. And then the bridesmaids will walk in one by one.

Everyone starts to sip up. And I hear the bagpipes. The little bugger! She knows I love the bagpipes and she's hired someone! Her grandad Russ, my Dad, loved the bagpipes. He died before Phil and I married. He was just 48. On the day of our wedding as I was getting ready upstairs at the hotel I heard the bagpipes. Phil had hired someone as a surprise. And here we are now, history repeating itself. I don't think I am the only one who enjoys the bagpipes, and as I stand to listen, I see a lot of the men stop in their tracks and listen too, no doubt having their own recollection of memories, good ones I hope.

The giant double doors open and again, the cheerful Master of Ceremonies, speaks. "Ladies and Gentlemen, the wedding will begin shortly. Please take a seat". The groomsmen are all looking very dashing and assist some of the older ladies into the room. It's not always well reciprocated now is it. The younger generation seem to often be insulted by acts of chivalry. Well not this lot. We love it. Good manners and etiquette go a long way in my book and all of these ladies are enjoying holding on to a strong arm.

The room looks absolutely beautiful. Everything and more I expected it to be. I can't wait for Es to see that her hard work in planning all of this has paid off. And then, the harpist begins. Almost our cue to go. Tom's nerves are beginning to show. He holds his mum's hand and his dads. They are all looking at one another with such love. He heads over to me and Jakes. The boys shake hands. Emotion written all over their faces. And then he holds my hand. Looks at me with his eyes brimming with tears and whispers "I love her so much" as he kisses my cheek. "I know you do. And she loves you". He heads through the double doors, making his way down the aisle and getting several fist pumps along the way. He is beaming. He looks even more handsome than usual.

Tom's parents now make their way to the doors. I see them recognise the music. Their wedding song. They look at one another and smile knowing full well it must have been Esme's idea to play this for them to walk into. I'm so bloody proud of my kind and thoughtful girl.

Jacob then does a pretty deep exhale, squeezes my hand and leads me down to our seats. I want to soak up every single bit. Some bits feel almost familiar. I've envisaged this for so long. It has got me through so many tough times etching this in my subconscious mind.

And then, I turn to look at the doors. Here comes the girls! One by one. Massive smiles, eyes glistening. They seem to float towards us. Every single one. Beautiful girls, inside and out. Beautiful friends to Esme. Beautiful members of our extended family.

Tom shuffles, I can see his hands fidgeting. Jacob used to do it all the time. In a crowded soft play, at his many school performances, on the *footy pitch. And I know Tom must be nervous, excited and everything in between. His best man pats him on the back. The music begins. I turn around to look at the doors again. And there they are. Standing still. Taking in the room before stepping inside. My brain is capturing the image, taking pictures. He looks really really handsome. And she is just perfection. Her little hand draped inside his arm. His huge hand on top of her hand. They look at one another and begin to make footsteps ahead of them. She has locked eyes with her groom. They are both so full of emotion and Tom wipes away the tears. I look to my husband and my daughter as they reach Tom. Phil has silent tears falling. Esme's lip is quivering. "You look beautiful darling" he says to his daughter, kisses her hand and then turns to shake Tom's hand. "She's all yours pal" he jokes before he comes to join me. I can feel his hand shaking. And he is pursing his lips to blow out his emotions. This is really happening. The readings from friends, the beautiful music. The giggles, the tears. And then it feels like no time at all before they are pronounced husband and wife and sharing their first kiss as Mr and Mrs.*

Their friends have never been a shy quiet bunch so when they're invited to clap their bride and groom, there are wolf whistles, cheers and whoops galore as Esme and Tom begin to lead the way outside. This definitely is THE BEST DAY EVER.

Princess

I arrived onto ward 40 and am greeted by none other than our besties daughter Abbie. Always such a lovely girl and now a lovely young woman. She was made to be a nurse. She checks with me if I am happy for her to look after me. I wouldn't want anyone else I tell her. She is so gentle and reassuring. She takes me into a room to do more of the pre-operative paperwork and to label me up. She explains that I won't come back here but will go to intensive care or high dependency. She then gives me a little well-being package that she has done for me herself as a gift but I barely get chance to look at it or show appreciation because everything starts to go bloody fast. There is no messing about here. Different surgeons come in, the anaesthetist team and then the theatres team. I immediately like this woman. Sally with a tan I called her. She is funny without being too much. She just makes me feel at ease and recognises how I am feeling. And then the next thing I'm in the bed being wheeled down to the theatres. I look back at Abbie and again give that very feeble wave I seem to do now as I swallow down the tears that are rising in my throat. I've had operations before so this shouldn't be new, but it is really overwhelming. I'm being wired up to everything and someone is telling me to make a fist and slapping the back of my hand. Everyone looks so busy but they all look across and smile as they see me. The anaesthetist is an old school chap with a grey ponytail. His demeanour reminds me of my dad which is comforting. But then I feel really really overwhelmed and the tears start. "I can't believe I'm having brain surgery. I'm so scared" I say to the anaesthetist in a squeaky voice that doesn't even sound like mine. "Princess, don't cry, let's get you to sleep". Definitely my dad, he's the only one who called me princess. And that's it. Lights out.

"Anna. Anna. You're in recovery lovely." I can hear a voice. And I look up to the prettiest face. And then I feel a massive pain in my head. I feel sick. I must be starting to retch. "I'm just going to give you something to help". And then I start to relax a bit. Mr A appears. Asks me some questions, tells me "very good" and heads off.

My nurse is lovely. And patient! She must think I am crackers. I am talking to myself – counting, reciting the alphabet, lifting up each limb and looking around. "It's all working Anna" she says. I tell her how scared I was that I wouldn't be able to be me again and that my poor husband was scared. She tells me that she will ring my husband soon to let him know I am out of surgery. It must have been a long day for him. He went to Chris and Claire's farm to dig up their field for them. I ask her the time and it is coming up to tea time. "Anna, is there anything you want me to say to him" she asks. "Tell him not to come in his gardening clothes and to bring me a flat white please". She looks at me confused and I tell her how I just want him to know I am still me and not to rush in getting here.

It felt like it was no time at all before I was up on the ward. High Dependency Unit as I was doing well and didn't need one to one constant care in ICU. My friend Lou was one of the first ones to see me. She's a dinky woman, half Indian with hair like Hagrid (her words not mine). Lou was my boss, and became my friend. Along with her husband Kristian. Now this is a couple that laughs together. Full on belly laughs and they are great to be around. We call Lou, Voodoo Lou as everyone she meets she feels like she knows them. She also goes for psychic readings, far too many, and believes everything that they say! I don't think she clicks on that they are on her Facebook and can see her life unfolding. We had some giggles when we worked with hospital volunteers along with Rachael. Proper belly laughs. Raucous nights out. Times that if I think about them it was like a television comedy sketch interviewing some very eccentric prospective hospital volunteers whether they were having a sip of morphine mid interview, declaring they just want to cuddle all the babies or thinking they would very soon be chief executive. I absolutely loved working with volunteers....all walks of life who want to give something back out of the goodness of their hearts.

That night was a weird one. I felt almost hyper from the steroids and adrenaline but knew I had to try and sleep.

The nurses certainly earnt their wages with some very confused patients trying to get out of their beds. At one point I tried to help another patient and realised I had a catheter in. I absolutely could not wait to get it out the next morning and nagged enough for them to give in first thing and whip it out. I had been so scared before of not being me but I thought I was billy big balls I did, waltzing down that corridor thinking "I've just had my skull taken off, my brain cut into and look at me". Got to the loo, felt dizzy, fell against the cardiac alarm and everyone came running to me. Not so billy big balls.

Everyone seemed to know I worked at the hospital. I think Deb and Claire had rang the ward to see how I was. I had only worked with them for a few months but they really did mother me which I liked! Just days before my surgery they knocked on my door unexpectedly. "Stand back Binks" Deb shouted "don't want to give you any germs" and then they placed gift bags on the doorstep. I didn't know what to say. I loved doing the collections and buying the gifts for others but to be on the receiving end. Wow. There was all sorts – a Jo Malone candle, didn't dare even light it…so posh! Gifts for the kids. And vouchers for a swish restaurant for when I was better. Honestly, you work at a hospital and there are so many good people you meet. Deb joked she would be scrubbed up ready for surgery and I half believed her. I mean, that would have been good.

I had a lot of "what do you do" questions from the staff. I had been so proud to work for the plastics team before I was in medicine. The surgeons were the best bunch of people. I think they had their own way of testing me a few times when I first started working with them and for them to see what I was about. And I am pretty sure I passed when they saw I was a do-er, not a sit at the desk and emailer. I loved sorting out the problems and trying to make things easier for them so they could focus on the important bits. And so when a couple of familiar faces came up to see me on the ward, I was very touched. Mr Milner who was surprised to see me in my hospital gown as thought I was working up on the 4th floor, not a patient. And Mr Haeney who complimented my shiner. All this kindness fuelled me with determination to get home. That and the fact that when I was sat eating my cheese salad for tea, there was a lady in the next bay to me literally behind her curtain having a poo on the commode.

Sun and Smiles

Phil and I follow Esme and Tom outside. It is such a nice day. Their photographer is briefing them on what is next. Phil is directing the champagne and canapes to Es and Tom. We have always been feeders. And they will need their tummies lining that's for sure. They are surrounded by their friends. Tom takes both glasses of champagne whilst Esme is busy chatting. "I need this" he says winking at me as he drinks both. She hates having her photo taken, very much like us, but also is her mama's girl and likes to capture all of the memories. My two used to spend hours looking over photos we had taken. Even from toddlers "show me when I lived in your tummy". We have always loved photos.

I have never seen so many people smiling and laughing. All dressed up and enjoying the weather, the occasion and the feeling of love we all seem to have. There are huge garden games set out and already some lads are having a game of chess. I can hear "so nice to see you" and "you haven't changed a bit" from people who now live at opposite sides of the country. It's a bloody proud moment seeing so many people turn up for your child.

I've always said, it's not often you get to have all your loved ones together so this for us is extra special as we celebrate our daughter becoming a woman, gaining a son and new friendships with our families. We manage to guzzle a glass of champagne before being herded to the vibrant gardens for our turn at photographs. Poor old Jacob was nominated to deliver messages from the photographer to get groups together – he's a tall lad like his dad but not always the loudest and certainly not with people he doesn't know well. "Mother! I don't even know who half of these people are. I haven't been sober most times I've met them" he is half whispering and half shouting. He's still a mummy's boy at heart and likes me to sort things out. And secretly I like it too. I end up going over to Rose. Rose is the dinky dot bridesmaid…my god that girl is a little pocket rocket. I used to do the school run with Amy, her Mum, and she is such a mix of her her and very musical dad. She takes no shit from anyone but has the softest heart and cheekiest sense of humour. I think has always had a soft spot for Jacob, and he for her too. "Jacob has no idea who half of the people are for photo's Rose, can you help him round people up please" I ask her with a wry smile on my face. She has always known that I adore her. I told her many a time on the way to dropping the girls off at drama class that both she and Jacob reminded me of two characters in an amazing series I watched years ago called "This is Us". She is Sophie and Jakes is Kevin....albeit a less troubled version I hope! As I head back to the crowd I hear her winding Jacob up already and look back to see my boy all coy. Maybe the best day ever is about to get even better.

"Daaaaaad"

"Daaaad, hurry". I can't work out who it is, Esme or Jacob. Sometimes they sound so similar. "I'm fine darling" I fight to say in between the retches. Both of them are pacing the landing. Phil had been giving Ted his evening walk and very suddenly the chemo side effects kicked in. I've never been a quiet puker but chemotherapy vomit is something else. I was on a combination called PCV – it was 3 different medications some intravenous and some tablet and even to this day the thought of swallowing those tablets makes me gip. It was literally burning me, fluorescent yellow coming out of my mouth and nose.

I had already shooed the kids away. The nurses had told me to be careful as the bodily fluids would contain the toxic drugs and was dangerous to others. There was no way any of them were going to be put in any danger so as hard as it was, I couldn't let any of them comfort me. There were cleaning wipes in almost every room. After almost turning my stomach inside out, when I just wanted to lay still, I'd be disinfecting instead. Phil gently approached the en suite door. "This is killing me Anna, I can't stand seeing this happen to you". "I'm sorry, I'm so sorry" I cried. "Just make sure they're ok Phil, play a game with them or something". And off he trotted. I knew he felt useless. But knowing he was there for them when I couldn't be made my treatment so much easier. In some ways I felt like I was prepping him for the future, for being a widower and single parent. Something that I couldn't bear the thought of but that I also had to be very realistic about. I'd encourage him to take them to his Mum's or go and play footie on the field. I used to sign up to girls' nights out which I really couldn't be arsed to go to but which I felt was important to make sure they had time on their own. I never dared say it out loud, but I was always conscious that I wanted to see them doing good together. I couldn't bear the thought of Phil withdrawing from them. Maybe drinking too much. Or snapping at them. All which would have been understandable in some ways. I knew myself after my Dad died, how I then worried about my Mum. And I didn't want them to have to become the adults looking after Phil. I wanted them to find a way together as my 3 musketeers. Whether it was her age or just her nature, Esme took on the stereotypical female role. She would help me with the dishwasher. She would make herself a wrap or pizza bagel as she called them. If she was in a good mood she sometimes even made her brother something. But I was always very alert to the fact that it isn't just a female role to simply cook and clean after people. In my day, we worked full time and juggled the housework, childcare, homework, school events, shopping, cooking… the lot as well as everything to do at work. Phil's Mum always used to tell me how lucky I was that he helped out and it used to rile me up something rotten. We were a team. If you're in any sort of a relationship, if you're a family or if you are simply house mates…everyone needs to eat, have clean clothes and tidy up after themselves. It's not a female role. It's everyone's home and everyone's role especially when there are two people working full time.

A Binks Banquet

The family and friends photographs are finished now and Phil and I stand watching our newly wedded daughter and our new official son in law. He keeps squeezing my hand. "You did good Anna" he says. He has always said this over the years. "WE did good babe" I reply.

The Master of Ceremonies has announced that the wedding breakfast will begin in 5 minutes. I really don't know why they call it a wedding breakfast. We were certainly not going to have guests go hungry. "If there's one thing I don't mind paying for, then it's a decent feed" Phil had told us when Esme and Tom first started wedding planning. We had been to many weddings over the years where he had still been hungry! We don't do hungry in our house so when it came to the tasting menu, Esme and Tom invited both sets of parents to have an input. The food was all bloody lovely. Phil likes a big hearty meal, meat, spuds and two sides where as I am a little and often type. Much like Esme (although she can still demolish a roast and go for seconds and thirds). With it being a summer wedding Esme and Tom chose a mix of both. And now my nerves are settling, I can't wait to get stuck in.

The main guests begin to head into the dining room. It looks magnificent. Glass topped circular tables with fairy lights underneath the glass and pressed flowers. Lazy susan's to spin instead of reaching across one another for the food. A pianist in the corner playing soft music. It really is pretty. We have to stay behind, as apparently it is now customary to introduce the more significant bridal party members. "American" Phil had complained when he feared that we would have to devise some sort of funky dance and make an entrance! He was reassured when Esme said absolutely not! She isn't shy, but she isn't loud either. She has always had etiquette and class that lass. But she wanted the main characters in her life to have an entrance too. My turn was to walk in with Tom's Mum. We linked arms and headed in, little shake of the hips here and there and found our seats. We were soon followed by the Dad's, one of which looked a bit pale ahead of his speech!

"Ladies and Gentlemen, please be upstanding for the newly weds" the Master of Ceremonies announced....and the crowd went off! Seeing my girl, and my new son, sashay through the tables, saying hello to each table as they went, brought back that emotional lump in my throat. "They really are something special aren't they" I whispered to Tom's Dad.

They had decided, to alleviate everyone's nerves, and make sure the mountain of food is eaten, to do the speeches first. Phil was up first. His voice is shaking. But he does brilliant if I do say so myself. A mix of him recalling his little girl growing up, a little bit of embarrassing her and a lot of pride and praise for both Esme and Tom. To top it off, he presses play on a remote control and a beautiful video begins. Many of our photos and videos of Es and everyone who loves her over the years. There isn't a dry eye in the room. He leans over to Tom, and says "I loved her first. I always will. I hope you both have a marriage full of love and laughter just like Anna and I have. I trust you Tom. Keep my girl feeling loved and make her laugh" as he leans in to shake his hand and give him a big bear hug. Esme has already risen from her seat. Her lip wobbling again. Her Dad's arms engulf her. I can't hear what is said but I can see their shoulders shaking with little sobs.

They sit back down and Tom checks first that his bride is ok. He pours Esme and him a glass of iced water. And he begins. His voice keeps faltering. He truly knows her. He truly knows all her good points and he is truly proud to be her husband. He is proud to join our family. He is proud to be Jacob's brother. They are going to have such a fun time together. Isn't that what it is all about – not just the lovey dovey stuff, the fun and laughter too. My god there will be hard times, but so long as they can laugh, they will get through those times. The rest of the speeches are a blast. The best man, the slide show of the stag do and the states they were all in. And even the bridesmaids do a little speech too.

And then Esme and Tom stand up together, holding hands, to thank

everyone for being here and then to thank us, their parents for everything we have done for them throughout their lives and in helping with the wedding. Tom has the remote control now and asks everyone to turn around and look at the screen. There he/she is. Their little baby who is growing safely. Both sets of parents already knew and had been sworn to secrecy. She was nervous, like any mum to be. But like her dad had said when I was pregnant after all that IVF. "it's going to be ok, you'll soon be newborn knackered". The roof almost blew off with the excitement. She stood to the side and rubbed the tiniest 16-week bump to a standing ovation. This is it.
This is all you can ever wish for, to be surrounded by people who are truly rooting for you.

You do you, I'll do me

But not everyone in your life do root for you.

There had been different tough times before the cancer diagnosis. Times before Phil and times with Phil. They say you don't always remember what someone has said to you but you always remember how someone made you feel. My friend Rachel for example. For a long time, I was the only one out of our group who didn't have children. And naturally during our nights out, there would be talk of their children. Their milestones, the latest problems they were presenting with from nursery bugs, sleepless nights or potty training. Of course there were, your children are the main focus of your life, so I never expected anything else and I actually enjoyed hearing about the joys, and the not so fun bits. I was always interested. And I always enjoyed the cuddles with their babies. I always watched and admired thinking if I got lucky, I will do that or won't do that. But at the times when I had a miscarriage or a negative cycle, it could be heavy knowing I was the odd one out. The way Rachel treated me made me feel seen and heard. She knew I loved babies and children. She knew I would make a good Mum. But she also knew that some days were hard. And, she said it out loud. I still remember her trying to direct the conversation away from kids when she thought things were bleak for me. And I remember her being so genuinely rooting for me.

Rachel was who I went on my girls first holiday with. Her family was very different to mine in some ways, but also similar in that there was a lot of love. Her parents were very successful in business but also very down to earth and supportive and guiding her. My parents' kind of let me get on with it which sounds great but there were also times I needed their wisdom and to be told! I paid for my own driving lessons and was chuffed with myself when I passed first time at 17. I remember my friend Kelly ringing from the pharmacy she worked at to find out how I got on and she celebrated my success more than anyone else. I think she must have known about the fun times we would have driving around. We went all over! Stalking ex boyfriends mostly. And then there was the time we took her Dad to yankee land drive through when he was very drunk. Great times.

Naturally, as I had passed my test, I wanted a car. But I didn't know where to start. I ended up getting myself a little Fiat Punto. White it was and the registration N156 KAT. Bloody loved that car. Those were the days that you could fill your tank for £30 and make it last a good few weeks. When I thought it was time to get a new car, Rachel and I went driving round show rooms on one Sunday. The sales man must have seen us coming and rubbed his hands together. I spotted a lovely little car I liked. Anyway, he sits me down and here I am signing up to some sort of finance where he just told me the monthly amount. I thought I could afford it. Left there buzzing that next week I would get my shiny car. Rachel must have been a bit nervous as she said we would go to her house. Her Mum and Dad were sat there relaxing after their Sunday lunch and in we walked with the signed paperwork. They took one look at it, read the small print and blew their top! Not at me but the garage. The interest rate was sky high and they were not impressed. Her Mum got on the phone and gave the salesman a talking to and cancelled the order for me. That's where Rachel got her tenacity from. And also her caring nature. They were such nice people and her Dad was hilarious. I still remember him showing me his watches and saying "these are Japanese" and pointing to his legs "and these are hairy knees".

And when I got ill, despite rarely seeing one another due to adult commitments, Rachel again validated me. How hard and scary things must be. She would send me a text telling me I was strong and she was proud of me. She would ask after Phil and the kids. Good human nature. I had lots of lovely friends who I adore to this day. But, as with all things, as well as the good, there were some ugly.

"She doesn't even look ill"

"she's young, she will get over it"

"is it even cancer"

"I wish I could have chemo, you are so thin"

"She's had it ages its nowt new"

"when are you going back to work"

God I heard it all. I am a very positive person and saw the very best in some people but also the worst in some people.

I had three of the loveliest managers when all of this happened. Wendy, Stephen and Lesley were amazing with me. Wendy sent me cards which I loved reading. They often had cute pictures on and Esme would pinch them to display them in her room. They had all vowed they would do everything they could to get me back at work and within the same role or one that was going to be better for me and my situation. I don't know about you but I had massive guilt being off sick. I was so worried about all these symptoms I had and worried that I would let them down if I agreed to go back. What if I had meetings and I couldn't lift my head off the pillow. One of the consultants asked if I had considered asking for ill health pension. I didn't even know that was possible at my age. But I went away and thought about it. And because I can't make a decision about what to do for tea let alone anything major like leave work I decided I would let the professionals decide. I told them to start the ball rolling. I didn't want to see any of the occupational health or the consultants reports because it was too scary for my mind to deal with so I literally left it to NHS Pensions and their specialists to decide.

And I got awarded an enhanced pension due to whatever had been written by the Neurosurgeon and Oncologist about my health and prognosis. I was both scared at what that meant for me health wise, I was sad that I was leaving my job and the Trust I had loved for 11 years but also glad that the decision was made and that I would now be at home for the children.

But some people hated it because I looked well and I didn't have to go to work. Don't get me wrong, I know how hard it was to work and have a family. Nursery costs, juggling holidays. So I was shocked when some people seemed to begrudge the fact that I could now do pick up, drop off and get to all the school performances. And didn't acknowledge that I actually had side effects, that I tried so hard not to show, from having my brain cut into and fried and the long term effects of chemotherapy.

Then there were the comments on my weight. I'd had comments on my weight being up, down and everything in between (I can confirm whatever size you are, you will still be your biggest critic). The chemo had made me very thin and very frail which didn't go unnoticed. "Don't lose anymore, you look ill". I am ill I thought. Maybe it was my fault. I didn't talk much about it - let's face it, no one wants to hear woe is me. Our lovely friend Boz helped us out, especially Phil, and became the one information giver at Phil's work (he had cried at work one day when asked about me and he was mortified). Most people were really intuitive and respected that I wasn't a talker but there were still a few people who didn't respect it. I was asked, when my children were by my side, has the chemo worked, what my prognosis was, has it shrank. Texts that simply said "what's the latest". So rude. I have had the more distant 'friends' ringing closer friends showing disdain because I didn't ring them with updates. I was even rudely and aggressively questioned by someone "why have you had chemo", "why have you had radiotherapy" and who when I confirmed it was indeed cancer, didn't think to say I am sorry to hear that or even, that must be hard, how are the children? In the end, the message got across to people. "If I want you to know, I will tell you".

One of the good things about my diagnosis is that I have grown in confidence in some ways. I no longer feel that I have to put my own feelings aside to protect others from feeling uncomfortable. I have never in my life wished anything but happiness for others but often I put my own happiness at risk for the sake of others. I can see the same traits of this in Esme and Jacob at times and try to instill in them that they must take care of themselves but be kind and take no shit either. I mean how do you even do that? In real life and in teaching your kids? I don't want my children having wakeful nights recounting certain conversations or situations or dreading potential interactions.

Of course I am not the only one to have tough times, my friends have suffered over the years and one thing I have learnt is that people will talk if they want to. You can get a gist of those who needs to, who wants to. You can get a gist of those who want to but don't know how to. You can get a gist of those who don't want to even mention it. Some people like to withdraw like a little tortoise for a few days, weeks even. And then poke their head out when they can face the world again. Others like to vent on social media. There is no wrong or right way. Just your way. Talk if they want to talk, but don't fire intrusive questions at them just because you're a nosey get or deem yourself so important that you should know everything.

You have different people in your life who know different versions of you. I think this is a good thing. We have the friends who you go out with, scream with laughter with, dance round your handbags with. You have your friends who catch you getting off the village bus from a hospital appointment and finds out when your next appointment date and time is and then turn up to your house to drive you there. You have your friends who you sit around the table with the kids playing cards. You have your school parents friends, who are there for your kids especially. You have your friends who you manage to meet twice a year in a coffee shop with. You have your work friends, thrown together as strangers, all ages, and end up like family. You have your text only or send funny videos with no accompanying message with. And most of them have certainly graced my life positively. I guess the message in this bit is don't be a dick. Don't say anything about anyone behind their backs that you would be uncomfortable with if they confronted you. And just let others do them and you do you. No one needs to be upset or offended. We are all so different. Different people, different couples, different families, totally different jobs, different homes, different finances, different hopes, different dreams. But that doesn't mean we can't respect or empathise with one another's differences. I've always maintained – it's just chemistry. Friendships, our relationships. We can't get on with everyone, we don't even always like everyone, but we can let them do them, and you do you. If you think about it, it's all like a bank account. If one side keeps taking and taking, then you are in the red. If you put in too, then you get back in the black. Give and take.

The Party

If it's one thing we do right, it is a party with people having fun. And Tom's family are on the same wavelength.

After the baby news was out, the atmosphere was even more full of excitement.

The food came out. Delicious cuts of meat, veggie and vegan options too. The potatoes – Phil's specialty of garlic roasted hasselback spuds that he told the chef in great detail of how to recreate...."they'll go down a storm mate" he exclaimed. Sweet potato wedges. Beautiful breads – olive and sun dried tomato being my favourite. And salads....not just a bit of iceberg, we are talking every colour of the rainbow salads, rice salads, pasta salads. The guest tables were buzzing with chatter and "try this one" "delicious" as they spin the lazy susans to get a bit of everything. I looked over to the table the Chapman's were on and laughed as Craig did the 'chefs kiss' action and winked. Definitely a success.

I watched my daughter, with child, walk around the tables of her guests absolutely beaming. Her friends asking if they can touch her dinky bump that was beginning to show. I watched my son deep in animated conversation with friends. And I watched my husband. My husband. My gorgeous husband who has given me a life that I could only dream of. My husband who has loved me as I deserved to be loved and who I have loved right back. My husband who has had me shedding tears of laughter and who has always said he loves it that he can make me laugh like that. My gentle husband who gave me two beautiful children who have grown into two beautiful adults. My husband that introduced me to an array of his fire service friends and those friends then becoming my family. My husband who has worked hard for us but also appreciated that I have worked hard for us too. My husband with whom without him, I wouldn't be me. I have envisaged this moment for so many years. When times were bleak. Dark, grey skies, rain on the windows bleak, the only thing that could keep me going was manifesting this moment. I would sit picturing Phil seeing Esme for the first time in her wedding dress. Picturing my son, my strapping gentle giant of a son, dressed in his suit with the girls' all making eyes at him. I could physically feel my husband's hand encasing mine. I could feel my sons' adult arms around me. I could feel my daughter's soft cheek against mine and inhaling her beautiful perfume. And I got here. They told me, they being the doctors, in 2021, around 3 to 4 years. Thank God the sun broke out of those bleak skies and helped me to picture this. Helped me to focus. Helped me to fight. And now, picture me. Picture me as Nana Anna. The fight doesn't end here.

The following pages contain information that you may find useful. Anything you don't feel comfortable with, just skim over. This is only my experiences and what worked for me. Like I said earlier, we are all different.

Some Tips for Cancer and Brain Tumour Patients

Emotions

First of all don't try to be anything other than you. You may not be the same you as you were before. You may mourn that you. You may be embracing the new you. For me it is important to be me in the midst of the very moment.

If I am tired, I nap.

If I am weepy, I cry.

If I am generally not feeling it, I retreat.

I dont hide as much anymore. I try to say how I feel. "I'm sorry, I'm knackered and grumpy. I'm off for a nap." "I just need to have a quiet few days, its nothing you've said or done".

You have every right to be angry. I am pissed off that this is still hanging over us. Not just the initial stages but the in between waiting of MRI's and the results. Analysing every twitch or pain. Seeing my husband worried, upset or annoyed at the situation. Seeing my kids worried. They do get on with their normal lives but even now at their young ages, they are conscious mum has cancer and that cancer kills.

You have every right to be hyper. I wanted to, still want to, get all the family experiences done. Eat beans on toast for a month so that we could go watch a big football game or go to a concert just to see the kids faces. Plan family days as often as possible. And also plan recovery days.

You have every right to ask questions. Of your medical team. For clarification. For hope. For information that contradicts what you might have researched. Sometimes medical staff are dealing with so many patients that they forget we are human. Don't be afraid to let them know you are a person, with hobbies, with families, with friends, with hopes, with aspirations and with worries.

You have every right to be concerned with your appearance. Hair loss, weight loss, weight gain, spots, bloated, twitches, seizures, fatigue, skin tone, feeling wobbly and having balance issues and needing aids such as walking sticks.

You have every right to take up the support on offer. I sometimes feel that the support available is for people much more poorly than I. There are counsellors, groups, advice around finances, practical support services such as transport to and from appointments, befrienders. People who will support your loved ones too. And of course, family and friends who want to help. I always find it hard to accept help from people I know, I am so used to being the one who helps others out. But I also realise that it helps friends to deal with the situation too. Let your family and friends do school pick ups, bring food, give you a lift somewhere.

You have every right to <u>not</u> take up the support on offer. Support groups can be a great place but also a hard place. Some people focus on the negatives. Some people get through it by posting all the bad bits. Including photos. This can be very triggering. I have deleted myself from many groups because of this. They can be a constant reminder. And it makes it hard for me to manifest those good things.

You have every right to doubt. I try to be positive all the time. I try to manifest all the good things. I dont know how to do it. Even now, am I doing it right? If you are going to doubt one thing, doubt the negative bits. They don't always get prognosis right. They are often based on historic and out of date statistics.

You have every right to <u>not</u> take the advice. Every man and his dog had a cancer antidote. With the very best intentions I am sure. My sisters friends uncles aunt....drank the juice of Glaswegian cherries and now doesn't have any evidence of cancer. You need to take this magic supplement, gently roasted on a bed of dock leaves from the amazonian rainforest. Every person who knows you have a cancer will offer you advice, send newspaper cut outs often of extremely costly, sell your house costly and still not enough, immuno treatment. You will get sent links to weird and wonderful supplements, told about someone who was riddled with cancer and now is 112 and still riding a bike. And you'll also get the people who will tell you about someone who has died from cancer. Died from 'your' cancer. Many of the miracle immuno treatments are not affordable for every day people. Some of the diets recommended are expensive or just plain stressful to adhere to.

You have every right to do what is best for you! My experience and thoughts will be completely different to yours. I just want you to be able to do what you want! We don't have much control over our health, but we can take back control of the here and now. Make your life as stress free as possible. I am still trying to figure it out. I love fruit and vegetables, but cant stomach drinking them. Surely eating them has to be just as good as drinking them....and besides, our teeth and tummies do the same as a blender so I count it as exercise and not relying on a device to do it for me!

Surgery

Surgeons are unique. Their skillset, their personalities, their backgrounds. In my experience of working and knowing surgeons, they are fixers. They simply see a problem and they fix it. My own surgeon once said to me "I am just the technician!". Undervaluing himself for sure. I am lucky to have worked with and been cared for some wonderful surgeons who have been very honest. Again, in my experience, you ask a surgeon or consultant a question and you get a very factual, evidence-based answer.

They have to tell you worst case scenario and all the risks when getting your consent for surgery.

They are human. Having been on the other side and working with surgeons I can tell you that they put their all into what they do. They want the operation to be a success. They want your recovery to be a success. They try their best. They discuss your case with other surgeons to get the best outcome for you, not just in the same hospital you are being treated at but sometimes colleagues they have met along the way in different areas, different countries even.

You may be given leaflets or advice on the surgery you will have. You may find there is nothing on the tv but cancer adverts or programmes with surgery in it. I have to admit that I am a need to know it all person. The good, bad and the ugly. I watched a craniotomy on youtube prior to my surgery. It did shake me a tad. But it also helped me because I had a reason behind the post surgery feelings and side effects I have.

Don't shave your hair! I was told on numerous websites and groups that shaving your hair would make it all more bearable and that doing it yourself was better than the surgeon doing it. I didn't and I advise you not to. Sure, the scars can be huge. Mine runs from my hairline above my eye down to my ear. And I cannot see one bit of it! I can feel the dodgy screw that sticks out but I cant see it. The surgeons undertake these operations day in day out.

And their stitching skills are better than your grannies darning skills. My surgeon had said that he wanted to do all that he could to avoid frightening my children. And as a result I woke up with a scar hidden in my hair line and my children never saw anything physical except a black eye.

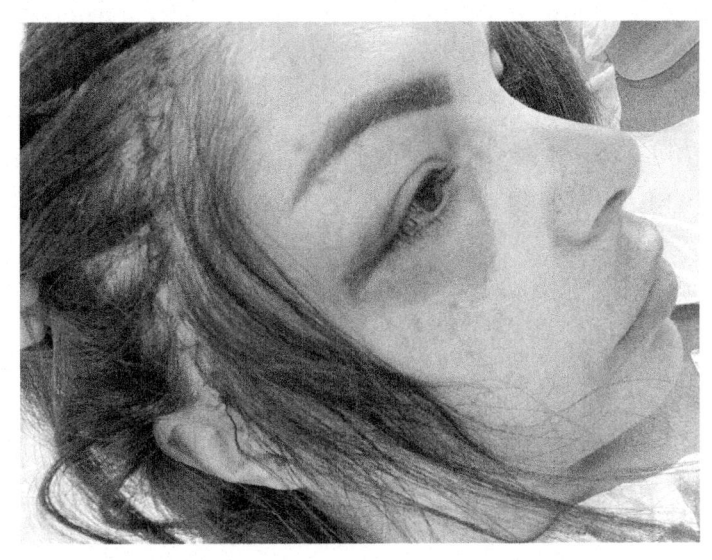

For your hospital stay you won't need much at all. Don't overthink it.

I would recommend taking:

Toiletry bag. Moisturiser and lip balm are a must.

Soft hair brush. You won't want to drag a brush through your hair and affect your wound healing but there might be some areas you can gently brush. You will also be advised to use baby shampoo on your return home when you can get your head wet so have some ready.

Baby wipes – quick swiff to mop away the whiff.

Soft mints or citrus sweets.

Your headwound, no matter how it is positioned or dressed, will be sore. Take button up nightwear to avoid putting things over your head. And even some button up clothing for coming home in.

There are a variety of smells on a hospital ward which can make you feel sick. You could mask these by having a roll on perfume to place on your wrist and sniff. Or even placing menthol on a hanky and sniffing that.

Ear plugs – unless you are medicated, you won't get much of a decent sleep. Ear plugs are a must.

Soft socks. Don't take any that will be tight, you can often swell whilst unwell.

Long dressing gown. You might end up wearing the open back gown for longer than you think if you are having scans etc. A long dressing gown is a must. No one wants their bum bobbing through the slit of a hospital gown.

A blanket. My beautiful friend Tess gifted me a lovely blanket with photos of Phil, the children and I on it. It was bloody lovely… definitely a comfort blanket. And my other gorgeous friend Jane printed a photo of us all for me to take in. They were the things that really brought comfort and focus.

I took snacks in, don't bother! You probably won't feel up to eating much and besides, our NHS is very generous. There are 3 meals a day plus coffee, tea or juice in between and the offer of a biscuit, cake or fruit. You will not go hungry!

PICTURE ME

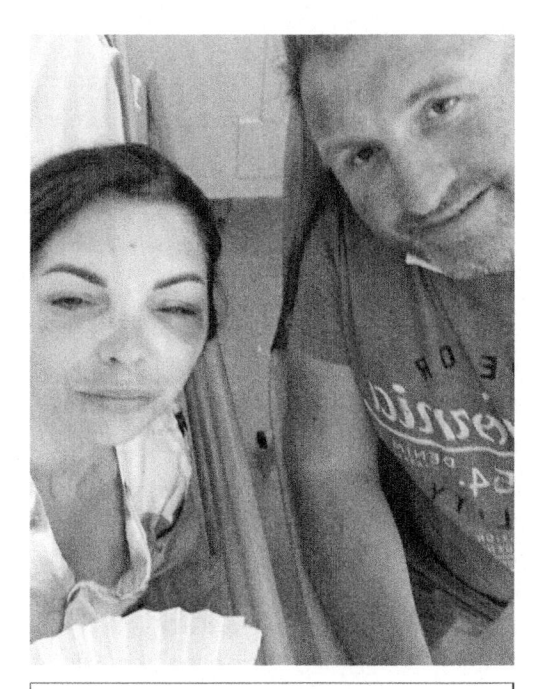

This photo was taken a few hours before I came home. Phil arrived and we set off for home. I was excited to do the school run. I happened to look in the back of the car, it was ram packed with rubbish....he had only decided that it was a good idea to whizz to the tip on the way home.

Radiotherapy

Radiotherapy was an odd one – intense and draining, for me anyway. I had to do a lot of meditation. I wasn't the humming and bahhhing type but in my mind I had to really focus and find a happy place to visualise.

I had 2. One was in the past and one was in the future.

The past one was a holiday to Greece for my 40th. Ikos Olivia. It was the most amazing resort and I hope one day to get back there. We were just happy. Nice food, clean, nice people and relaxed beyond belief. So focussing on that was easy. I got so into it I could hear the splashes of the pool, feel the warmth of the sun. It was lovely. I still visualise this now on the tough days.

And of course, the future happy place is Esme's wedding. As you have just read about (I should actually say to Es here….you dont have to get married! Be who you want to be darling…so long as you dont identify as a cat. I cant change your litter tray sorry babe).

Radiotherapy wasn't undertaken until six months post surgery for me. This was to prevent wound breakdown. I only had 60 percent of the tumour removed due to it's position so I was keen to crack on and try and get rid of the rest.

With radiotherapy you have to get measured up for a bespoke mask. For me, I had a planning appointment. They scan your head in different areas and then plan the route for the laser. It is completely painless. But, it is very claustrophobic.

The making of the mask was also very claustrophobic but if I can do it, you can definitely do it. You lay on a table and they bring out a sheet of plastic which has holes in. They soak it in hot water to make it pliable and then you have a member of staff either side of your head who place it on your face and push it down over your face and head. Your natural instinct is to try and fight it! I literally had to give myself a good talking to. Keeping still and going with the flow is really important so that they can get the mask right and get the planning right to hit the tumour. I calmed myself completely down, flared my nostrils to make the breathing easier and told myself it was all to get better. Your mask is kept at the hospital whilst you have your treatment. I had six weeks of daily radiotherapy and I was allowed to take the mask home afterwards which entertained the kids.

Again, I was warned of hair loss. And again I asked shall I shave my head. Some people did, some didn't. Because of my surgery experience I thought I would wait.

There are long waits associated with radiotherapy. Waits in corridors/areas where other patients are. Some who like to talk, some who can be quite intrusive with their questions and some who are clearly very poorly from a variety of cancers. You would be wise to take in a book or headphones to listen to music or a podcast. For me, the machines would break down often and the waits would be longer so a book was a must, and it stopped people talking to me when I couldn't be bothered for small talk!

When you are called through to the therapy room, there is a machine which looks like a donut – like the MRI or CT scan you will have had however this one has super beams to come out of it!

The member of staff will confirm your details and then get your mask. You lay on the bed and they ask if you are ready. Once you say yes they place the mask on your face and head and then clip it into place. You can't move because of this and it is claustrophobic. I fought the urge to say "I'm a celebrity get me out of here" and imagined those happy places. The member of staff quickly leaves you and as soon as they have, their colleague at the computer end matches the beam to where it needs to go and presses the go button. The actual beam part is over very quickly hence why I say imagine your happy place and breathe through it. As soon as it is over (literally a few minutes) the member of staff was back to release me.

You then leave the treatment room. I always wanted to get straight out of there but you can have a breather and a rest. You will find that some days you swell and the mask feels tighter. The holes in it also make a funny pattern on your face which can get a few looks as you leave the hospital!

I waited for the hair loss. We got to week 4 and I got a bit cocky and thought well I'm not going to lose it. And then wham into week 5 and I had an area the size of a large hand which was as smooth as a baby's bum. Very luckily, as my treatment was directed to the temporal lobe area and I had a lot of hair, it was able to be hidden underneath the top part of my hair. Except for when it was windy and then it looked like I was wearing a toupe and it was flapping in the wind.

The kids absolutely hated my bald spot. They used to say "just when I had got it all out of my mind and now it brings it back". Which I totally understood. I was much more chilled about this patch of hair and found it quite relaxing to stroke the area. It felt lovely! I had always had thick hair. I didn't expect for it to grow back but it did, and fast. Literally six months later my hair was back there fully. It was perhaps a little bit thinner, and had a wave to it, but it was there. I know for a lot of people hair is really important to them so if you are about to embark on radiotherapy please don't make any drastic decisions about cutting or shaving it off.

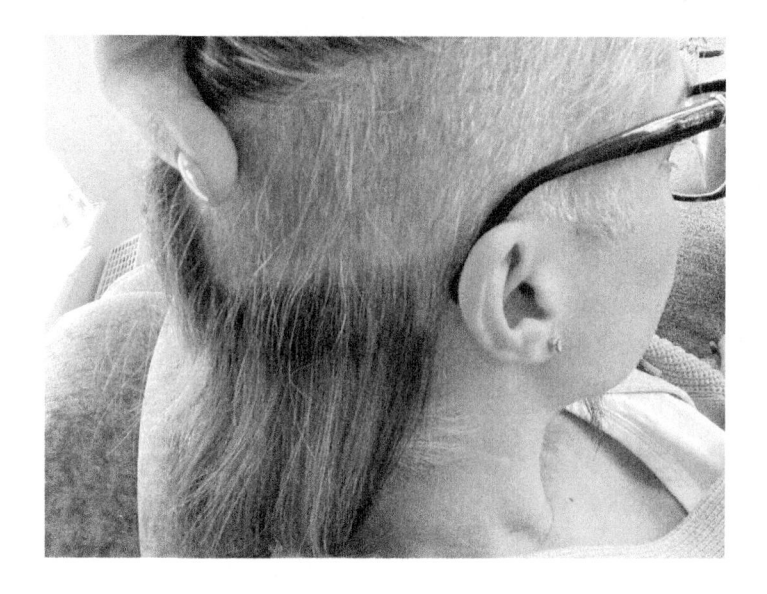

Another thing to note for both surgery and radiotherapy is that you are not allowed to drive. I surrendered my drivers licence before my surgery. There was no way I was putting anyone in danger in case I had a seizure whilst driving.

Providing your surgical recovery goes well, you can apply for your licence after a year. If you then have to have radiotherapy you have to reapply for your license. They write to your Consultant too. Different tumours and different grades will affect the duration of time that you are not allowed to drive for. The DVLA website will have more information depending on your diagnosis.

I have to say, not having my independence was one of the worst parts. I live in a village with poor public transport so it was especially hard. I regained my licence once treatment was done and I had shown no signs of neurological decline and the first thing I did was go to Home Bargs for a mooch – pure bliss!

The last day of each treatment can be a really big thing for patients. Some people choose to stop and ring the bell and acknowledge how hard it had been and recognise the fact that they got through it. People take photos, videos. I considered it but decided it wasn't for me and sloped off.

Chemotherapy

Chemotherapy, again, hair loss is expected. I couldn't wear the cold cap, absolutely no way. I'm a cold arse anyway let alone wearing a freezing cap strapped to my head. But my thick hair genes were stronger than the chemo. It thinned out but it still looked fine. Which was lots of comfort for Esme and Jacob. And of course I didn't get the pitiful stares that people often give to those who are going through cancer. That must be really tough if you are like me and don't like people feeling sorry for you.

A massive side effect of all 3 chemo types I had was extreme fatigue. And it doesn't go away. So in the acute stages of treatment, sleep as much as you can. My mum always said that sleep would heal you and I fully took that advice. I can remember hot sunny days listening to the kids playing in the garden and just falling into a really nice restorative sleep. If you push yourself too hard you end up paying for it for days afterwards so I do advise nana naps!

I had an allergic reaction to one of the chemo's I was on. I rang the helpline and was told to just monitor it however luckily I had my friend Kelly who worked there (and who was a godsend in getting me medication sorted and answers to questions quickly) and I had friends Hayley and Marie who are ward sisters. I sent photos of the allergic reaction to them and all agreed it didn't need monitoring it needed seeing to and told me to ring back and name drop! Very quickly I was admitted. Hayley even came and collected me from home and took me in and settled me on the ward. It took around a ten days with steroids and anti inflammatories to get sorted.

For chemotherapy, the obvious side effects are sickness. If one anti sickness doesn't suit you or work then ask for another one. And always take them even when you don't feel sick. It will help trust me. I did worry about not being able to get enough vitamins in me. I bought some sachets called Meritene. The chocolate milkshake was my favourite. They're designed for the older generation to get their vitamins and minerals in and they taste lovely! I whizz mine up with water and ice and it tastes like a McDonalds shake. If you are losing a lot of weight you might want to make it with your milk of choice.

I also guzzled ice cold water. I haven't fancied it since but during chemo I loved it. On the days where fluids are hard to swallow, ice pops can help. If holding them in your hand is too cold, you can wear an oven glove! Phil once crushed up a load of ice pops for me and put them in a big glass and gave me a spoon. It was so refreshing and definitely helped.

I ate chewy mints. Wherever I went I had a packet of soft mints. They just helped refresh my mouth and take away the metallic taste.

You may lose a lot of weight during chemo. I certainly did. Part of me quite liked the thin experience as I was always a womanly figure shall we say. But when I look back on photographs now I can see why so many others were concerned. So eat what you can, when you can. But keep yourself hydrated. Infection wise, my bloods weren't great, infact they were pretty poor but luckily I never got seriously unwell. This was with children who were at school picking up every bug. Just be sensible. We washed hands religiously, we kept everything clean. Friends and family should be understanding. I often had people tell me that they were feeling sniffly so would stay away.

My other side effects, whether it be from the treatments above or the medication I was then put on, range from developing autoimmune issues, painful hands, joints, off the chart fatigue, headaches, high blood pressure, poor memory and sensory problems. My left side doesn't work properly I wobble and lean to that side. The list is endless but again, I listen to my body and go with the flow. You can over think every ache and pain but don't wind yourself up. Keep your medical team updated and they can offer an appointment or reassurance.

Scans

The worrying will always be there. You will have regular MRI's. They are every 3 months for the first year. If things remain stable they go to every 4 months and then up to 6 months.

I have MRI spectroscopy scans and am now at every 4 months. These measure the chemicals in your brain too. All very clever.

The room you have your MRI done in is freezing! Wear warm clothes and without any metal at all. I usually wear a soft crop top bra, leggings and a hoodie. And warm socks!

You are cannulated as they attach you to a robot which injects the contrast solution in to highlight the tumour. You lay on the hard bed and the staff will place ear plugs in your ears and chunky comfort pads at the side of your head before placing a grill type thing over your head and face. It doesnt touch your face like the radiotherapy mask. This is to keep you still. But it is still quite claustrophobic. They give you a buzzer to hold incase you really cant bear it. Just try to visualise good things and keep still. Some people fall asleep, I am very envious!

Depending on which machine is used, there is sometimes a mirror as you head through into the tunnel. This can be a good thing or a bad thing. I often cant help but look and I see staff pointing at what they are seeing on the screen. They are not allowed to tell you a thing! When I once questioned, after my scan, what they were pointing at, I was met with "we could have been choosing our lunch!".

The scan duration varies, but for me it has always been between 60 and 90 minutes (it was nigh on 120 minutes for the surgery planning scan!). They talk to you through a microphone from their room and speaker near you in the machine. Luckily they have always spoken to me and told me how many minutes each scan sequence is so it kind of helps me to count down. I visualise - usually that nice holiday to try and warm me up. And sometimes

I sing songs in my head to try and shut out the magnets clunking.

Once your scan is completed you will have a breather and wait for around 15 minutes. If you are feeling ok they will take the cannula out and you can be on your merry way.

Brain MRI's are very intricate. They go through every slice of your brain images. And results can take a while (in Hull they are around 6 - 10 weeks at present). They then need to be discussed at the MDT. This can be a really anxious time. Scanxiety is real! The nights can be long. I take Amitriptyline which helps me sleep. It is only the lowest dose but it does help. You will find your own way of dealing with it. I cant lie, each time can be different. I have had scans where the previous one has shown signs of tumour activity, increased blood flow, something of concern. And so waiting on results is awful. Again, it is a case of finding what helps you – plan activities, meditate, manifest, listen to podcasts…write a book!

Life Stuff

I wanted to get things in order just in case.

I put all of my bank items in a folder along with pension paperwork. Also the kids bank accounts.

We renewed our wills and gave a copy to our executors. We made sure our house was legally the children's in the event of either of us passing away. This brought a lot of comfort for me knowing things were in order.

Unfortunately I didn't have any life insurance. I had a small life insurance through my NHS employment with a reputable company (BHSF) however, like many people, I had paid religiously and they found something in the small print to not pay out. I appealed this but failed. They did at least give me my contributions back but I felt very cheated.

I pay for my funeral upfront by monthly direct debit. This isn't direct with a funeral director but through a health and wellbeing company.

Holiday insurance can be very difficult to get. And very expensive. There are often people in the newspapers who have had a illness or accident abroad and are crowd funding to get back home for treatment. I would never dare go abroad without insurance. As much as I would love to take the kids to Disney in America, the insurance is ridiculously high! So we stick to the trusty caravan or European holidays. The company I have used and been happy with is Insurance With. I would advise you to shop around. And please be completely honest with the questions they ask. No minimising things to get a cheaper quote.

My lovely husband thinks the loft will cave in at some point because of the things I like to save for the kids. I think it is nice to have things from your childhood when you are older and one of the best things are the photographs you take whilst making memories. Printing photographs isn't that common now but I use an app called photobooks where I just upload photos from the phone on a regular basis and get an album sent to us. You can put blank pages in too and write more about what you were doing in that particular photograph which is nice. I always think when you look at a photo, it can take you straight back to that very moment and just make you feel happy. Try and make sure you get in the photographs too, I have a habit of capturing everyone else. You will never regret taking photographs.

Thank you again for buying this book and for taking the time to read it. I hope to keep going, and keep making memories.

Printed in Great Britain
by Amazon